A Brief History of Russia:

From Kievan Rus to Soviet Union and beyond

Marc Ferrari

COPYRIGHT

A Brief History of Russia: From Kievan Rus to Soviet Union and beyond
Copyright © 2023 by Marc Ferrari
All rights reserved.

QUOTE

"Whatever the mind of man

can conceive and believe,

it can achieve"

Russian Proverb

Table of Contents

SETTING THE STAGE FOR RUSSIA'S RICH HISTORY   7

KIEVAN RUS: THE BIRTH OF A NATION   10

MONGOL RULE AND THE EMERGENCE OF MOSCOW 13

THE RISE OF THE ROMANOVS AND THE TSARIST ERA
18

THE TIME OF TROUBLES: CHALLENGES TO THE
TSARIST REGIME   24

PETER THE GREAT AND THE WESTERNIZATION OF
RUSSIA   27

CATHERINE THE GREAT AND THE GOLDEN AGE OF
RUSSIAN CULTURE   30

ALEXANDER I AND THE NAPOLEONIC WARS   33

THE DECEMBRIST REVOLT AND THE PUSH FOR
REFORM   37

THE EMANCIPATION OF THE SERFS AND THE RISE OF
INDUSTRIALIZATION   40

THE RUSSO-JAPANESE WAR AND THE REVOLUTION OF
1905   43

WORLD WAR I AND THE RUSSIAN REVOLUTION OF
1917   47

THE BOLSHEVIK REVOLUTION AND THE FOUNDING OF
THE SOVIET UNION   54

STALIN'S RULE AND THE RISE OF TOTALITARIANISM 57

WORLD WAR II AND THE GREAT PATRIOTIC WAR   59

KHRUSHCHEV'S THAW AND THE DE-STALINIZATION OF THE SOVIET UNION   61

BREZHNEV'S STAGNATION AND THE END OF THE COLD WAR   65

THE COLLAPSE OF THE SOVIET UNION AND THE EMERGENCE OF RUSSIA AS A NEW STATE   67

PUTIN'S ERA AND THE RESURGENCE OF RUSSIAN POWER   70

REFLECTIONS ON RUSSIA'S PAST AND FUTURE PROSPECTS   74

SETTING THE STAGE FOR RUSSIA'S RICH HISTORY

Russia is an incredibly diverse and complex country, with a rich and varied history that spans over a thousand years. From the earliest days of the Kievan Rus to the present day, Russia has undergone many transformations and has had a profound impact on world history.

It all began in the 6th century AD, when the first Slavic settlements were established in what is now Russia. But it wasn't until the 9th century that the foundation of modern Russia began to take shape with the emergence of the Kievan Rus. This early state was centered in the city of Kiev and ruled by a prince or Grand Duke, who controlled a loose federation of tribes and principalities.

Over the centuries, the Kievan Rus expanded its territory and became an important center of trade and culture, with Kiev serving as a hub for commerce and art. The influence of the Byzantine Empire, which spread Christianity to the region, was also profound, and Kiev became a center of religious learning and art.

However, in the 13th century, the Mongol Empire invaded and conquered the Kievan Rus, ushering in a long period of Mongol rule that lasted until the late 15th century. During this time, Moscow emerged as a center of power, and the Grand Dukes of Moscow gradually expanded their territory and consolidated their rule over the surrounding regions.

The 16th and 17th centuries saw the emergence of the Tsars of Russia, who claimed descent from the Grand Dukes of Moscow. They continued to expand their territory and develop their autocratic rule. Ivan the Terrible, who ruled from 1547 to 1584, is perhaps the most infamous of the Tsars, known for his brutal policies and campaigns against his own people.

But there were also many notable achievements during the Tsarist era, including the reigns of Peter the Great, who modernized Russia and made it a major European power, and Catherine the Great, who presided over a golden age of culture and art.

The 19th century saw growing calls for reform and liberalization in Russia, culminating in the Decembrist Revolt of 1825, which was swiftly put down by Tsar Nicholas I. The Emancipation of the Serfs in 1861 was a major step towards modernization, but it also brought about new challenges and tensions within Russian society.

The 20th century was marked by revolution, war, and political upheaval. The Russian Revolution of 1917 brought the Bolsheviks to power and led to the establishment of the Soviet Union, which would dominate Russian politics for much of the century. The Soviet Union saw many notable achievements, including industrialization, victory in World War II, and advances in science and technology, but it was also marked by authoritarianism, repression, and human rights abuses.

The collapse of the Soviet Union in 1991 was a momentous event in Russian history, leading to a new era of political, economic, and social change. Today, Russia is a complex and multifaceted nation, grappling with its past and charting a course for its future.

In the chapters that follow, we will explore the many facets of Russia's rich history in greater detail, from the earliest days of the Kievan Rus to the present day. We will examine the key events, people, and ideas that have shaped Russia over the centuries, and seek to understand the unique identity and culture of this fascinating nation. So come along on this journey and let's dive into the history of Russia together!

KIEVAN RUS: THE BIRTH OF A NATION

The story of Russia begins with the Kievan Rus, a loose federation of tribes and principalities that emerged in the 9th century in what is now modern-day Ukraine. The Kievan Rus served as the precursor to modern-day Russia, and its foundation marked the beginning of the country's rich and diverse history.

The origins of the Kievan Rus are somewhat shrouded in mystery, but historians believe that the early Slavic tribes that inhabited the region began to form alliances and federations in response to the threat posed by the nomadic tribes that roamed the Eurasian steppes. These federations were often led by a prince or Grand Duke, who acted as the nominal leader of the various tribes and principalities.
The first recorded leader of the Kievan Rus was **Rurik**, a legendary Viking warrior who is said to have been invited to rule the region by the Slavic tribes in the late 9th century. Rurik established himself as the ruler of Novgorod, a powerful city-state located in the north of the region, and his descendants would go on to rule over the Kievan Rus for several centuries.

The story goes that in the late 9th century, the various Slavic tribes inhabiting the region were in a state of constant warfare and disunity. Seeing an opportunity to gain power and wealth, Rurik and his fellow Vikings, known as Varangians, sailed down the Dnieper River and established a fortified settlement at Novgorod. From there, they gradually expanded their control over the surrounding territories and established a new state, which became known as Kievan Rus.

While the precise details of Rurik's life and achievements are impossible to verify, there is little doubt that he played a significant role in the early history of Kievan Rus. Under his leadership, the various Slavic tribes were united under a single ruler, creating a sense of political cohesion and stability that had previously been lacking. Rurik is also credited with establishing the princely dynasty that would rule over Kievan Rus for the next several centuries.

Despite his accomplishments, Rurik remains a somewhat enigmatic figure, with much of his life and legacy shrouded in legend and myth. Some accounts suggest that he was a fierce warrior and a skilled politician, while others depict him as a more benevolent figure who brought peace and stability to the region.

Under the leadership of the Kievan Rus, the region experienced a period of growth and prosperity. Kiev, the capital of the federation, served as a center of trade and culture. The Rus traded extensively with Byzantium and other parts of Europe, and the region became a hub of commerce and art. Christianity was introduced to the region by the Byzantine Empire, and the Kievan Rus became a center of religious learning and art.

The most notable ruler of the Kievan Rus was Vladimir the Great, who ruled from 980 to 1015. Under Vladimir's leadership, the Kievan Rus expanded its territory and consolidated its rule over the surrounding regions. Vladimir was also responsible for the Christianization of the Kievan Rus, which led to the construction of many churches and monasteries and the spread of literacy and education throughout the region.

However, the Kievan Rus began to decline in the 12th century, as a series of internal conflicts and external pressures began to take their toll. The region was repeatedly invaded by nomadic tribes from the steppes, and the various principalities of the Kievan Rus began to fight among themselves for control and influence.

In the 13th century, the Kievan Rus was conquered by the Mongol Empire, which ushered in a long period of Mongol rule that lasted until the late 15th century. While the Kievan Rus would eventually fade into obscurity, its legacy would endure. The various principalities that had made up the federation would eventually coalesce into a single, unified state that would come to be known as Russia.

Today, the legacy of the Kievan Rus is still visible in many aspects of Russian culture, from its religious traditions to its art and architecture. The Kievan Rus marked the birth of a nation and laid the foundation for the rich and varied history of Russia that was to follow. It is a fascinating story of how a loose federation of tribes and principalities came together to form a nation, and it serves as a reminder of Russia's deep and complex roots.

MONGOL RULE AND THE EMERGENCE OF MOSCOW

The period of Mongol rule in Russia is a fascinating chapter in the country's history, one that laid the foundation for the emergence of Moscow as a center of power and influence. The Mongol Empire swept through the region in the mid-13th century, conquering most of modern-day Russia and establishing a system of principalities.

In the 13th century, the Mongol Empire under Genghis Khan began its expansion into Eastern Europe. The Mongols, who were known for their military prowess and nomadic lifestyle, conquered much of Asia and Eastern Europe, including Russia. The Mongol invasion of Russia, also known as the Mongol-Tatar invasion, had a significant impact on Russian history and society.

The Mongol invasion of Russia began in the 1230s when the Mongol army led by Batu Khan, a grandson of Genghis Khan, crossed the Volga River and began conquering the Russian principalities. The Mongols quickly captured several key cities, including Kiev and Novgorod, and forced the Russian princes to pay tribute.

The Mongol rule in Russia was characterized by a centralized system of government, with the Mongol Khan serving as the ultimate authority. The Russian princes were allowed to rule their principalities as long as they paid tribute to the Mongol Khan and provided military support when needed.

Under the Mongols, Russia was organized into a system of principalities, each ruled by a prince who was appointed by the Mongol Khan. The Mongols were relatively hands-off in their governance of Russia, allowing the princes to maintain a degree of autonomy as long as they paid tribute to the Khan and provided soldiers for his armies. Despite this, the period of Mongol domination was marked by widespread devastation and hardship.

The Mongols exacted heavy taxes and tribute from the Russian princes, which often led to widespread poverty and economic stagnation. The Mongols also brought with them a culture of violence and warfare, which further destabilized the region and led to frequent conflict and bloodshed. This was a time of great challenge and adversity for the people of Russia, who struggled to maintain their way of life amidst the chaos and destruction.

However, despite the challenges of Mongol rule, a new power was emerging in Russia: the city of Moscow. Under the leadership of **Ivan Kalita**, the prince of Moscow, the city began to consolidate its power and expand its influence throughout the region. Moscow was strategically located at the confluence of several major rivers, which made it an ideal center of trade and commerce.

Ivan Kalita was a significant figure in the history of Russia and played an important role in the formation of the

Moscow principality. He was the Grand Prince of Moscow from 1325 to 1340, and his reign marked the beginning of Moscow's rise to power and prominence in Russia.

Ivan Kalita was born in 1288, the son of Prince Daniel of Moscow. He was named Ivan after his grandfather, who had been the Prince of Vladimir. When his father died in 1303, Ivan became the co-ruler of Moscow with his older brother, Yuri. Together, they worked to strengthen their principality, expand its territory, and increase its wealth.

One of Ivan Kalita's most significant achievements was his successful negotiation with the Mongol rulers, who had been dominating the region since the 13th century. In 1328, Ivan was able to secure a treaty with the Mongols that recognized Moscow's autonomy and granted it the right to collect taxes on behalf of the Mongol rulers. This agreement allowed Moscow to strengthen its economy and consolidate its power within the region.

Under Ivan's leadership, Moscow also became a significant religious center. He founded the Cathedral of the Archangel Michael in the Kremlin, which became the burial place for Moscow's rulers. He also supported the construction of other churches and monasteries in and around Moscow, further solidifying its religious importance.

Ivan Kalita was also a patron of the arts, commissioning many works of art and literature during his reign. He sponsored the creation of the illuminated manuscript known as the Sophia Psalter, which was considered a masterpiece of medieval Russian art.

Despite his many accomplishments, Ivan Kalita's reign was not without challenges. He faced opposition from other Russian princes who were vying for power, as well as from neighboring states such as Lithuania and Novgorod. However, he was able to maintain his position and continue the growth of Moscow's power and influence.

Ivan Kalita died in 1340, leaving behind a legacy of a strong and prosperous Moscow principality. His descendants would go on to play a significant role in the history of Russia, including his grandson Dmitry Donskoy, who famously defeated the Mongols in the Battle of Kulikovo in 1380.

Ivan Kalita worked tirelessly to strengthen the position of Moscow within the Mongol Empire. He paid tribute to the Mongol Khan and provided soldiers for his armies, but he also worked to build alliances with other Russian princes and consolidate his power within his own principality. Over time, Moscow emerged as the preeminent city in Russia, and its rulers began to see themselves as the natural heirs to the legacy of the Kievan Rus.

The emergence of Moscow as a center of power and influence was aided by several factors. The city's strategic location at the crossroads of several major trade routes made it a hub of commerce and wealth. Its rulers were also savvy political operators, adept at playing the various factions and interests of the region off against one another.

Finally, Moscow was able to take advantage of the chaos and instability of the Mongol period to consolidate its power and expand its territory.

By the end of the 15th century, Moscow had emerged as the dominant power in Russia. Its rulers, known as the Grand Princes of Moscow, had successfully consolidated their power and expanded their territory, and they were poised to take the next step in Russia's evolution: the establishment of a centralized, autocratic state.

Despite the challenges of Mongol rule, this period in Russian history was also marked by significant cultural and artistic achievements. The Orthodox Church, for example, flourished during this time, and many of Russia's most famous churches and cathedrals were built during the Mongol period. Russian literature and art also began to develop, with works like "The Tale of Igor's Campaign" and the icons of Andrei Rublev representing significant contributions to the cultural landscape of the time.

The period of Mongol rule in Russia was a difficult and challenging time, marked by widespread poverty, violence, and instability. However, it was also a period of significant cultural and artistic achievement, and it laid the foundation for the emergence of Moscow as a center of power and influence. The story of Ivan Kalita and the rise of Moscow is a testament to the resilience and determination of the Russian people, who persevered through some of the most difficult times in their country's history.

THE RISE OF THE ROMANOVS AND THE TSARIST ERA

The Romanov dynasty, which ruled Russia for over three centuries, is a fascinating period in Russian history filled with dramatic events and notable achievements. The Romanovs ascended to the throne at a time when Russia was still an undeveloped country struggling to keep up with its European neighbours. However, by the time they were overthrown, they had transformed Russia into a major world power.

In 1613, Russia found itself in a state of turmoil after a period of instability known as the Time of Troubles. It was a time of foreign invasion, famine, and civil war that had left the country devastated. The people were in desperate need of a strong leader to bring stability and order back to the land. That leader came in the form of **Michael Romanov**, who would go on to become the first tsar of the Romanov dynasty.

Michael Romanov was born in 1596 to a noble family that had been exiled to the remote village of Galich by Ivan the Terrible. His father, Feodor Romanov, died when Michael was only a year old, and his mother, Xenia Shestova, raised him on her own. Michael's upbringing was modest, but he received a good education from his mother, who was an intelligent and educated woman.

In 1612, after the end of the Time of Troubles, a national assembly was called to elect a new tsar. The assembly selected Michael Romanov, who was just 16 years old at the time, to be the next leader of Russia. The decision was not without controversy, as Michael was seen as young and inexperienced by some. However, his family's ties to the previous ruling dynasty and his reputation for being honest and just won him the support of the assembly.

Michael's reign was not without challenges. He inherited a country that was in a state of disarray, with widespread poverty, corruption, and lawlessness. He also faced threats from the neighboring Polish-Lithuanian Commonwealth, which had designs on Russian territory. Michael knew that he needed to establish his authority quickly if he was to have any hope of restoring order to the land.

One of Michael's first acts as tsar was to create a new legal code that would govern the country. The code was based on the principles of justice and fairness and aimed to bring order to the courts and the legal system. Michael also worked to improve the economy, encouraging foreign trade and supporting the development of new industries. He knew that a strong economy was essential to the stability of the country.

Michael was a relatively unknown and inexperienced ruler, but he quickly set about consolidating his power and establishing the foundations of the Romanov dynasty. One of his first acts was to establish a new system of government in Russia, which replaced the traditional nobility of the boyars with a new class of nobles who were loyal to the tsar. This new class of nobles, known as the dvoryanstvo, would play a crucial role in shaping the course of Russian history in the centuries to come.

The early years of the Romanov dynasty were marked by relative political stability and prosperity. Michael and his successor, Alexis, worked tirelessly to modernize Russia and bring it into the mainstream of European politics and culture. They reformed the legal system, established a standing army, and built new cities and infrastructure. They also worked to expand Russia's territory, conquering Siberia and pushing Russia's borders eastward.

The reign of Peter the Great, who ascended to the throne in 1682, marked a turning point in Russian history. Peter was a visionary and ambitious ruler who was determined to transform Russia into a major European power. He embarked on a program of modernization and westernization, introducing reforms to the military, government, and economy. He built a new capital city, St. Petersburg, which he modeled on the great cities of Europe. He also embarked on a series of military campaigns that extended Russia's territory and influence throughout Europe and Asia.

Despite the successes of Peter's reign, the Romanov dynasty faced significant challenges and setbacks in the 18th century. The later years of the century saw a series of wars and political crises that weakened the dynasty and undermined its legitimacy. The reign of Catherine the Great, who came to power in 1762, was marked by political intrigue, corruption, and repression.

However, the Romanov dynasty persevered, and it continued to shape the course of Russian history well into the 20th century. The 19th century saw the emergence of new movements and ideas in Russia, including the Decembrist uprising of 1825 and the populist movement of the 1870s. These movements reflected the growing dissatisfaction of many Russians with the autocratic and repressive rule of the Romanovs.

The Romanov dynasty finally came to an end in 1917, with the outbreak of the Russian Revolution. The Bolsheviks, led by Vladimir Lenin, overthrew the provisional government and established a new socialist state. The Romanovs were deposed and eventually executed, bringing an end to one of the longest and most consequential dynasties in world history.

The last Romanov tsar, Nicholas II, came to the throne in 1894, succeeding his father Alexander III. He faced numerous challenges during his reign, including the 1905 Revolution, which saw workers and peasants rising up against the government. In response, Nicholas II was forced to concede some power to the newly formed Duma, Russia's first elected legislative body.

However, the tsar's attempts at reform were largely unsuccessful, and the outbreak of World War I in 1914 only added to the country's problems. The Russian army suffered heavy losses on the Eastern Front, while at home, food shortages and inflation led to widespread discontent. In February 1917, protests broke out in Petrograd (now St. Petersburg), fueled by the growing sense of disillusionment with the war effort and the government's inability to address the country's economic and social problems. Nicholas II was eventually forced to abdicate, and a provisional government was established in his place. However, the provisional government's authority was tenuous at best, and it was soon challenged by a radical socialist faction known as the Bolsheviks, led by Vladimir Lenin. In October 1917, the Bolsheviks staged a coup and seized power, marking the beginning of the Soviet era.

Nicholas II and his family were initially held under house arrest in the Ural Mountains, but in July 1918, they were transferred to a house in Ekaterinburg. On the night of July 16-17, a group of Bolsheviks entered the house and executed the tsar, his wife Alexandra, and their five children.

The execution of the Romanovs marked the end of not only the dynasty but also an era of Russian history. The country was plunged into further turmoil in the years that followed, as the Bolsheviks consolidated their power and established the Soviet Union. The Romanovs' legacy, however, lives on, with their story inspiring countless works of literature, art, and film, and serving as a reminder of the fragility of power and the consequences of political upheaval.

The rise of the Romanovs and the tsarist era marked a pivotal period in Russian history, one that transformed Russia from an undeveloped country into a major world power. The Romanov dynasty faced numerous challenges and setbacks, but it persevered and left an indelible mark on the course of Russian history. The story of the Romanovs is a testament to the resilience and determination of the Russian people, who have faced adversity and overcome it time and time again.

THE TIME OF TROUBLES: CHALLENGES TO THE TSARIST REGIME

The Time of Troubles was a period of immense turmoil in Russian history, and it had a lasting impact on the country's political and social structures. Following the death of Tsar Fyodor I, the last of the Rurik dynasty, in 1598, Russia plunged into a period of political instability and chaos. The various factions in the Russian court began vying for power, and this led to the emergence of several pretenders to the throne.

One of the most notable pretenders was False Dmitry I, who claimed to be the son of Ivan the Terrible. He was briefly recognized as the new tsar, but his reign was marked by violence and instability. He was eventually overthrown and killed in a rebellion led by Vasily Shuisky, one of the most prominent boyars (nobleman) in the Russian court.

The Time of Troubles was also characterized by economic crisis and social unrest. The wars and political instability of the period had a severe impact on the Russian economy, leading to inflation, famine, and widespread poverty. The suffering of the population was further exacerbated by the fact that many peasants and serfs were forced to flee their homes in search of food and shelter. This led to the growth of banditry and criminality, making life even more challenging for ordinary people.

The social unrest during the Time of Troubles culminated in a series of peasant uprisings and rebellions. One of the most significant of these was the Bolotnikov Rebellion, which began in 1606 and was led by the Cossack leader Ivan Bolotnikov. The rebellion was fueled by peasant grievances over taxes, land rights, and serfdom. Although the rebellion was eventually suppressed, it marked a turning point in Russian history, signaling the growing discontent of the Russian people with the tsarist regime.

The Time of Troubles also had a significant impact on Russia's relations with its neighbors. The wars and political instability of the period weakened Russia's position in Europe and Asia, and its neighbors took advantage of the chaos to expand their own territories. Poland and Sweden both invaded Russia during the Time of Troubles, and Moscow was briefly occupied by the Polish-Lithuanian Commonwealth.

The end of the Time of Troubles came with the election of Michael Romanov as the new tsar in 1613. Michael was chosen by a national assembly of nobles, who hoped that he would bring stability and order to Russia. Michael's reign marked the beginning of the Romanov dynasty, which would rule Russia for over three centuries. The Romanovs restored stability to Russia and implemented reforms that helped modernize the country.

The Time of Troubles remains an important period in Russian history, one that shaped the course of the country for centuries to come. It was a time of immense hardship and suffering for the Russian people, but it also provided an opportunity for them to voice their discontent with the tsarist regime. The Time of Troubles demonstrated the importance of strong leadership and stable governance in times of crisis and highlighted the need for Russia to modernize and strengthen its economy and military if it was to compete with its more powerful neighbors in Europe and Asia.

PETER THE GREAT AND THE WESTERNIZATION OF RUSSIA

Peter the Great's reign in Russia was marked by a deep-seated desire to modernize and westernize the country. Born into a Russia that was still largely isolated from the rest of Europe, Peter was keenly aware of the challenges his country faced in the face of growing pressure from neighboring powers such as Sweden, Poland, and the Ottoman Empire. He knew that if Russia was to survive and thrive in the face of these threats, it needed to embrace the cultural, economic, and military innovations of Western Europe.

One of the most visible manifestations of Peter's vision was the construction of a new capital city, St. Petersburg, on the banks of the Neva River. The city was built in a marshy area, and the construction process was difficult and arduous, with workers often suffering from disease, hunger, and exposure to the harsh elements. But Peter remained committed to his vision, and the city soon became a bustling hub of commerce, culture, and political power.

In addition to founding St. Petersburg, Peter implemented a wide range of other reforms designed to modernize Russia. He abolished the traditional Russian calendar in favor of the more accurate Gregorian calendar used in the rest of Europe, and he introduced Western-style dress codes, including the requirement that men shave their beards. He also created a state monopoly on alcohol, which helped to generate revenue for the state and curb drunkenness among the population.

Perhaps Peter's most significant reforms, however, were in the military and economic spheres. He established a standing army and navy, reorganized the military hierarchy, and introduced new training methods and tactics. He also encouraged the growth of a merchant class and established new trade routes, which helped to boost the Russian economy and reduce the country's dependence on agriculture.

Despite Peter's successes, his reforms were not without controversy. Many Russians saw them as a betrayal of traditional Russian culture and values, and there were numerous uprisings and rebellions during his reign. Some of the most notable of these included the 1698 Streltsy Uprising, which was sparked by Peter's attempts to modernize the military, and the 1707 Bulavin Rebellion, which was fueled by resentment over Peter's policies toward the Cossacks.

Nevertheless, Peter's reforms had a profound impact on Russian society and culture. They helped to break down the isolation that had characterized Russia for centuries and paved the way for a more integrated and interconnected Russia. They also laid the groundwork for the country's emergence as a major European power in the 18th and 19th centuries.

Today, Peter the Great is remembered as one of the most important figures in Russian history, a visionary leader who helped to shape the course of Russian history for centuries to come. His legacy continues to be felt in Russia today, both in the culture and architecture of St. Petersburg and in the country's ongoing efforts to modernize and adapt to a changing world.

CATHERINE THE GREAT AND THE GOLDEN AGE OF RUSSIAN CULTURE

Catherine the Great, born Sophia Augusta Frederica, is widely regarded as one of the greatest rulers in Russian history, and her reign marked a turning point in Russian culture and politics. Born in Stettin, Prussia, in 1729, Catherine married into the Russian royal family in 1745 when she wed Grand Duke Peter, the heir to the Russian throne. However, Peter proved to be a weak and unpopular leader, and Catherine eventually led a coup d'etat to remove him from power and claim the throne for herself in 1762.

During her reign, Catherine set out to modernize and westernize Russia. She was a staunch advocate of the principles of the Enlightenment, which emphasized reason, individual rights, and progress. She believed that by implementing Enlightenment ideals, Russia could become a more prosperous and powerful nation. Catherine made significant efforts to bring Russia into the modern world, both culturally and politically.

One of Catherine's most significant achievements was the expansion of the Russian Empire. Under her leadership, Russia acquired vast territories in the south and west, including parts of Poland, Finland, and the Crimea. These acquisitions helped to solidify Russia's position as a major European power and opened up new opportunities for trade and commerce. Catherine also implemented a number of reforms designed to strengthen the country, including improving the military, streamlining the bureaucracy, and promoting trade and industry.

In addition to her political reforms, Catherine was a patron of the arts, and her reign is often referred to as the Golden Age of Russian Culture. She supported many artists, writers, and musicians, and her court became a hub of artistic and intellectual activity. Some of the most notable figures she supported include the writer Alexander Radishchev and the composer Dmitry Bortniansky. She also founded the Smolny Institute, a school for young girls that provided education in the liberal arts.

Catherine's commitment to the principles of the Enlightenment extended beyond her political and cultural reforms. She was a strong advocate for religious toleration and abolished torture and capital punishment in many cases. She also established a code of laws that promoted the idea of equal treatment under the law. These reforms helped to transform Russia into a more modern and just society.

Despite her many achievements, Catherine's reign was not without controversy. She faced challenges from both within and outside of Russia, and she was criticized by some for her personal life, which was marked by numerous affairs and scandals. Nevertheless, her legacy as a patron of the arts, a champion of the Enlightenment, and a successful ruler has endured to this day.

Catherine the Great's reign was a pivotal moment in Russian history. Her commitment to the principles of the

Enlightenment helped to modernize and westernize Russia and transformed the country into a major European power. Her patronage of the arts and commitment to cultural and intellectual growth left a lasting legacy that continues to be felt in Russia and around the world. Catherine the Great remains a celebrated figure in Russian history, and her reign is widely regarded as a golden age of culture, progress, and enlightenment.

ALEXANDER I AND THE NAPOLEONIC WARS

Alexander I was a remarkable figure in Russian history, whose reign was characterized by significant achievements and challenges. Born in 1777, he was the eldest son of Grand Duke Paul, who was assassinated in 1801, paving the way for Alexander to ascend to the throne. At the time of his coronation, Russia was facing a turbulent period of uncertainty and political upheaval, which would shape the course of Alexander's reign.

One of the most significant challenges faced by Alexander was the threat of Napoleon Bonaparte, who was rapidly expanding his empire across Europe. At the beginning of his reign, Alexander pursued a policy of neutrality, hoping to avoid involvement in the ongoing wars that were ravaging the continent. However, as Napoleon's power grew, Alexander realized that Russia could no longer afford to remain neutral. In 1812, Napoleon launched a massive invasion of Russia, which would come to be known as the Patriotic War.

Napoleon's invasion of Russia in 1812 is often considered one of the most disastrous military campaigns in history. Despite initially achieving some success, Napoleon's army ultimately suffered a crushing defeat at the hands of the Russians, leading to his eventual downfall.

The French Emperor's decision to invade Russia was motivated by a number of factors. First and foremost, he sought to punish Tsar Alexander I for his refusal to comply with the Continental System, a trade embargo designed to weaken Britain. Additionally, Napoleon hoped to expand his empire further east and saw Russia as a potential ally or vassal state.

In June 1812, Napoleon's Grand Armée, consisting of over 600,000 soldiers, began its invasion of Russia. The Russian army, under the command of Mikhail Kutuzov, initially engaged in a strategy of retreat, burning their own crops and cities to deprive the invading army of resources. The two sides finally met in September at the Battle of Borodino, the bloodiest single day of the Napoleonic Wars, in which both sides suffered heavy casualties.

After the battle, the Russians continued their retreat, refusing to engage Napoleon's army in open battle. This tactic, combined with the harsh Russian winter and the lack of supplies, began to take its toll on the French army. Many soldiers died from starvation, disease, and exposure, and morale began to plummet.

By the time Napoleon's army reached Moscow in September, the city was largely deserted and in flames. The Tsar's troops had burned it to the ground, leaving nothing for the French to occupy or use as shelter. Despite this setback, Napoleon refused to abandon the campaign and instead stayed in Moscow for over a month, hoping to negotiate a peace settlement with the Russians.

But as the winter set in, the French army was increasingly isolated and vulnerable. The Russians, meanwhile, were able to regroup and begin a counteroffensive, attacking the French supply lines and harassing their troops. By November, Napoleon realized that he could not sustain his army through the winter and ordered a retreat.

The retreat proved even more disastrous than the initial invasion. The Russians pursued the French, constantly attacking their weakened and disorganized ranks. The French suffered heavy casualties from the cold, starvation, and disease, with some estimates suggesting that over 400,000 soldiers died during the campaign.

By the time Napoleon's army finally retreated across the Niemen River into Polish territory in December, it had been reduced to a fraction of its original size. The invasion of Russia had been a catastrophic failure, and it marked a turning point in the Napoleonic Wars.

Despite facing overwhelming odds, Alexander's leadership proved decisive in the war against Napoleon. He rallied the Russian people behind him, and his determination and military skill were instrumental in the eventual defeat of Napoleon's army. Alexander's victory was a turning point in the Napoleonic Wars and marked a significant moment in the history of Russia and Europe.

In addition to his military accomplishments, Alexander was also responsible for a series of internal reforms aimed at modernizing the country and improving the lives of ordinary Russians. One of his most significant achievements was the abolition of serfdom, which had been a longstanding social and economic institution in

Russia. The reform was met with some resistance from conservative elements within Russian society, but Alexander's determination and leadership helped to ensure its success.

Another notable achievement of Alexander's reign was the expansion of the Russian Empire. He acquired new territories in Europe and Asia, including Finland, Bessarabia, and parts of the Caucasus. This expansion helped to consolidate Russia's position as a major European power, and laid the foundations for future territorial and political developments.

Alexander's reign was not without controversy, however. He faced criticism from some quarters for his liberal policies, and his efforts to reform the country were met with resistance from conservative elements within Russian society. He also faced challenges from nationalist movements in Poland and other parts of the empire.

Despite these challenges, Alexander's legacy as a successful leader and visionary reformer has endured to this day. His contributions to the Napoleonic Wars and the Congress of Vienna helped to shape the course of European history, and his internal reforms helped to modernize the Russian state and improve the lives of its citizens. Alexander's reign marked a significant moment in the history of Russia and the wider world, and his legacy continues to be felt today.

THE DECEMBRIST REVOLT AND THE PUSH FOR REFORM

The Decembrist Revolt of 1825 was a significant moment in Russian history that had a profound impact on the country's political and social landscape. It was a culmination of the growing discontent among the educated elite and military officers with the Tsarist regime and the desire for political reform and liberalization.

The aftermath of the Napoleonic Wars had left Russia with a sense of vulnerability and unrest, with the country facing economic difficulties and growing social tensions. The death of Tsar Alexander I in 1825 created a power vacuum and sparked political turmoil, with different factions vying for power and influence. The Decembrists, a group of liberal-minded officers, seized the opportunity to push for reform and mobilized their forces to overthrow the new Tsar, Nicholas I.

The Decembrist Revolt was the first significant attempt to challenge the autocratic Tsarist regime and push for political change in Russia. The Decembrists were inspired by the ideals of the French Revolution and the liberal movements that were sweeping across Europe at the time. They believed in the importance of individual freedom, rule of law, and a constitutional monarchy, ideas that were ahead of their time in Russia.

The rebellion was short-lived, as the Tsar's forces quickly put down the uprising and arrested the leaders of the revolt. The Decembrists were tried and sentenced to death or exile, and many were sent to Siberia, where they lived in exile for the rest of their lives.

Despite the failure of the Decembrist Revolt, it had far-reaching consequences for Russian society. The crackdown on the Decembrists led to a wave of repression and censorship that stifled political dissent and opposition in Russia for decades. However, it also inspired a new generation of intellectuals and activists to push for political and social change in Russia.

The Decembrist Revolt marked the beginning of a new era of political consciousness in Russia, as many people began to question the legitimacy of the Tsarist regime and demand more rights and freedoms. It also gave rise to the Slavophile movement, which rejected the liberal ideals of the Decembrists and sought to promote a uniquely Russian form of nationalism and cultural identity. The Slavophiles believed that Russia should reject Western models of liberal democracy and instead focus on its traditional cultural and religious values.

Despite the setbacks of the Decembrist Revolt, the push for political reform and liberalization continued to grow in Russia throughout the 19th century. A series of reformist Tsars, including Alexander II, introduced limited constitutional reforms and abolished serfdom. However, these reforms were not enough to satisfy the growing demand for political freedom and social equality.

The Decembrist Revolt remains a significant moment in Russian history, as it marked the beginning of a long struggle for political and social change in the country. The legacy of the Decembrists lives on in the ongoing struggle for political freedom and social equality in Russia today. Their bravery and sacrifice continue to inspire people around the world who are fighting for democracy and human rights.

THE EMANCIPATION OF THE SERFS AND THE RISE OF INDUSTRIALIZATION

The Emancipation of the Serfs in 1861 was a watershed moment in Russian history that had far-reaching social, economic, and political consequences. The serfs, who made up a significant portion of the Russian population, were legally tied to the land and were effectively treated as property by their landlords. They had no legal rights, no say in their own destiny, and were subjected to harsh working and living conditions. The Emancipation Act granted them freedom and legal rights for the first time in centuries.

The Emancipation Act was a result of growing pressure for reform and liberalization in Russia. The reformist Tsar, Alexander II, recognized that the system of serfdom was outdated and unsustainable, and that reform was necessary for the country's economic and social development. The Emancipation Act was a radical step towards modernizing the Russian economy and society, but it was not without its challenges.

The emancipation of the serfs had significant social and economic consequences for both the peasants and the nobility. The peasants were granted their freedom, but they were also burdened with debt and forced to pay exorbitant redemption fees to their former landlords for the land they were granted. This led to widespread poverty and economic hardship among the newly-freed serfs. However, despite the challenges, the Emancipation Act gave the peasants a newfound sense of autonomy and self-determination. They were no longer tied to the land or beholden to their landlords, and they had the right to seek work and better opportunities wherever they could find them.

The nobility, who had relied on the labor of their serfs for centuries, were also affected by the Emancipation Act. Many were forced to sell their land to pay off their debts and adapt to the new economic reality. The end of serfdom also led to the rise of a new class of wealthy landowners and industrialists, who capitalized on the new opportunities presented by the freed labor force.

The Emancipation Act was followed by a period of rapid industrialization and modernization in Russia. The new class of landowners and industrialists invested in factories and infrastructure, and the country experienced a period of unprecedented economic growth. The expansion of the railway network and the development of new industries helped to modernize the Russian economy and bring it into closer alignment with the Western powers.

However, the rapid industrialization also brought with it new challenges, including labor unrest and social inequality. Workers in the new factories were often subjected to harsh working conditions and low wages, leading to the rise of labor unions and socialist movements. The growing disparities between the wealthy industrialists and the impoverished peasants and workers also fueled resentment and social unrest.

The Emancipation Act and the rise of industrialization marked a significant period of transformation in Russian history. The end of serfdom and the emergence of a new class of landowners and industrialists helped to modernize the Russian economy and society, but it also brought with it new challenges and social tensions. The legacy of the Emancipation Act and the rise of industrialization continue to shape Russian society and economy to this day.

THE RUSSO-JAPANESE WAR AND THE REVOLUTION OF 1905

The Russo-Japanese War was a significant event in Russian history that had far-reaching consequences. It was a conflict between the Russian Empire and Japan over territorial ambitions in East Asia, particularly in Manchuria and Korea. The war was triggered by a dispute over control of the Liaodong Peninsula and the Russian establishment of a naval base at Port Arthur in 1898.

The Japanese military was well-organized, well-trained, and had modernized its army, while the Russian army was plagued by corruption, inefficiency, and a lack of modernization. The war was fought on land and sea, with major battles taking place in Manchuria and on the coast of Korea. The Japanese scored a series of decisive victories, which culminated in the Battle of Tsushima in May 1905.

The Battle of Tsushima, fought on May 27-28, 1905, was a major naval battle of the Russo-Japanese War, in which the Imperial Japanese Navy (IJN) decisively defeated the Russian Navy. The battle marked the first time a non-Western power had defeated a Western power in a modern conflict, and it demonstrated the rising power of Japan and the declining power of Russia.

The battle was fought near the Tsushima Strait, which separates Korea and Japan, and was the final engagement of a long and bloody war between Russia and Japan. The Russian Baltic Fleet, commanded by Admiral Zinovy

Rozhestvensky, had sailed halfway around the world to reinforce the Russian Pacific Fleet, but it was intercepted by the Japanese fleet under Admiral Togo Heihachiro in the Tsushima Strait.

The Russian fleet was poorly prepared and poorly equipped, with outdated ships and inadequate training. In contrast, the Japanese fleet was modern and well-trained, with better tactics and more advanced technology, including wireless telegraphy and torpedoes. The Japanese had also blockaded the Russian port of Vladivostok, preventing the Russian fleet from receiving supplies or reinforcements.

The battle began on May 27, when the two fleets spotted each other and opened fire. The Japanese quickly gained the upper hand, using their superior speed and maneuverability to outflank and outgun the Russian ships. The Japanese also employed innovative tactics, such as using torpedo boats to attack the Russian fleet at night, and deploying mines to disrupt the Russian formation.

The Russian fleet suffered heavy losses, with over 20 ships sunk or captured, and thousands of sailors killed or wounded. The Japanese suffered relatively few losses, with only a few ships damaged and several hundred casualties. The battle marked a turning point in the war, as it effectively destroyed the Russian Navy's ability to project power in the Pacific.

The Russian navy suffered a crushing defeat, losing almost its entire fleet and effectively ending the war.

The loss of the war was a humiliating blow to the Russian Empire, which had hoped to expand its territory and influence in Asia. It also exposed the weaknesses and backwardness of the Russian military and state. The Russian people were outraged by the heavy losses suffered by their troops and the incompetence and corruption of the military leadership. This led to widespread protests and unrest, culminating in the Revolution of 1905.

The revolution was a complex and multifaceted movement, with various groups and organizations united by their discontent with the tsarist regime. It was characterized by strikes, protests, and uprisings across the country, as well as acts of terrorism and political violence. The movement had a significant impact on Russian society and politics, as it challenged the authority of the tsarist regime and demanded greater political representation and democracy.

The Revolution of 1905 ultimately failed to overthrow the tsarist regime, but it did force the government to make significant concessions. In October 1905, Tsar Nicholas II issued the October Manifesto, which promised greater political freedoms, including the creation of an elected parliament, or Duma. Although the Duma had limited powers and was subject to government interference, it represented a significant step towards greater political representation and democracy in Russia.

The events of the Russo-Japanese War and the Revolution of 1905 marked a turning point in Russian history, as they exposed the weaknesses and flaws of the tsarist regime and sparked a wave of reform and revolution. The Russo-Japanese War highlighted the need for modernization and reform in the Russian military and state, while the Revolution of 1905 demonstrated the growing demand for political freedoms and democracy. These events laid the groundwork for the revolution of 1917 and the eventual downfall of the tsarist regime.

WORLD WAR I AND THE RUSSIAN REVOLUTION OF 1917

The events of World War I and the Russian Revolution of 1917 were the catalysts for major changes in Russia's history, leading to the overthrow of the tsarist regime and the establishment of the Soviet Union.

At the outbreak of World War I, Russia entered the conflict as an ally of France and Britain, hoping to gain territory and prestige. However, the war quickly turned into a disaster for Russia, with heavy losses and insufficient resources leading to widespread discontent among the population. The strain on the Russian economy and military also exacerbated existing social and political tensions.

In February 1917, a popular uprising in Petrograd (now known as St. Petersburg) led to the abdication of Tsar Nicholas II, ending the Romanov dynasty's 300-year rule. The Provisional Government, led by Alexander Kerensky, took control of the country, promising democratic reforms and an end to the war. However, the government struggled to implement its reforms, and its policies failed to address the growing unrest among the working class and peasants.

In October 1917, the Bolshevik Party, led by **Vladimir Lenin**, seized power in a coup d'état, overthrowing the Provisional Government and establishing a socialist government. The Bolsheviks promised to end the war, redistribute land to the peasants, and transfer power to the workers and peasants through the establishment of Soviet democracy.

The Bolsheviks faced opposition from both domestic and foreign forces, leading to a brutal civil war that lasted until 1922. The Red Army, led by **Leon Trotsky,** emerged victorious, and the Soviet Union was officially established in 1922. The Soviet government began implementing policies aimed at industrializing and modernizing the country, as well as eliminating opposition to its rule.

The events of World War I and the Russian Revolution of 1917 marked a turning point in Russia's history, leading to the establishment of the Soviet Union and the rise of communism as a major political and economic ideology. The revolution also had far-reaching consequences for the rest of the world, leading to the formation of the Soviet bloc and shaping the geopolitical landscape for decades to come.

Vladimir Lenin

Vladimir Lenin was a Russian revolutionary and politician who played a crucial role in the Bolshevik Revolution of 1917, which led to the establishment of the world's first communist government. He was born on April 22, 1870, in the city of Simbirsk, now known as Ulyanovsk, in Russia.

Lenin's early life was marked by tragedy, with the execution of his older brother for plotting to assassinate Tsar Alexander III. This event had a profound impact on

Lenin, who became increasingly radicalized in his political views. He became involved in revolutionary activities and was eventually arrested and exiled to Siberia.

In 1917, Lenin returned to Russia from exile and led the Bolshevik Party in a successful revolution against the Provisional Government. He became the first leader of the Soviet Union and implemented policies aimed at transforming Russia into a socialist state. These policies included the nationalization of industry and the redistribution of land, which were meant to eliminate social and economic inequality.

The number of people killed during Vladimir Lenin's government in Russia is a matter of significant debate among historians, as precise records are difficult to obtain and many factors influence the estimates. However, it is widely accepted that tens of thousands, if not hundreds of thousands, of people were executed or died in prisons and labor camps during Lenin's rule.

Lenin led the Bolshevik Party in the October Revolution of 1917, which overthrew the Provisional Government and established Soviet power. In the years that followed, Lenin and the Bolsheviks instituted policies that were designed to consolidate their power and promote their vision of socialism. These policies included the nationalization of industry and agriculture, the establishment of state control over the economy, and the suppression of political opposition.

One of the most notorious episodes of Lenin's rule was the Red Terror, a period of intense violence and repression that began in 1918 and lasted for several years. During this time, the Bolsheviks conducted mass arrests, executions, and deportations of real or perceived enemies of the regime. The exact number of people killed during the Red Terror is unknown, but estimates range from 10,000 to 100,000.

Another factor that contributed to the loss of life during Lenin's government was the Russian Civil War, which began in 1918 and lasted until 1922. The conflict pitted the Bolsheviks and their allies against a loose coalition of anti-Bolshevik forces, known as the Whites. The war was marked by widespread violence and atrocities committed by both sides, and it is estimated that between 7 and 12 million people died as a result of the conflict and its aftermath.

It is important to note that the question of how many people were killed during Lenin's rule is a controversial one, and estimates vary widely depending on the source and methodology used. Some scholars argue that the number of deaths attributed to Lenin's government has been exaggerated by anti-communist propaganda, while others believe that the true number of victims is much higher than official figures suggest.

Under Lenin's leadership, the Soviet Union faced many challenges, including a civil war and famine. Lenin's policies were often controversial, and he was criticized for his authoritarianism and his use of violence to suppress political opposition.

Despite these challenges, Lenin remained a popular leader in the Soviet Union and was widely respected as a revolutionary and political thinker. He died on January 21, 1924, at the age of 53, and was succeeded by **Joseph Stalin** as the leader of the Soviet Union.

Leon Trotsky

Leon Trotsky, born Lev Davidovich Bronstein in 1879, was a Russian revolutionary and Marxist theorist who played a prominent role in the Bolshevik Revolution of 1917 and the early years of the Soviet Union. Trotsky was a brilliant orator and writer, and his ideas on revolutionary politics and theory helped shape the course of the 20th century.

Trotsky was born to a wealthy Jewish family in Yanovka, Ukraine. He became interested in revolutionary politics at a young age, and was involved in various Marxist groups throughout his youth. In 1898, he was arrested for revolutionary activities and exiled to Siberia, where he continued to organize and agitate.

After being released from exile in 1902, Trotsky became a leading figure in the Russian Social Democratic Labour Party (RSDLP), a Marxist political party that would later split into the Bolsheviks and Mensheviks. Trotsky's ideas on revolutionary theory and tactics differed from those of

Vladimir Lenin and other Bolshevik leaders, and he was initially seen as an outsider within the party.

Despite his initial differences with the Bolshevik leadership, Trotsky played a key role in the success of the Bolshevik Revolution in 1917. He was a powerful orator and writer, and his advocacy for a "permanent revolution" and his criticisms of the moderate Mensheviks helped rally support for the Bolshevik cause.

In the early years of the Soviet Union, Trotsky was a prominent figure in the government and military. He played a key role in the establishment of the Red Army, and was appointed Commissar of Foreign Affairs in 1917. However, his growing disagreements with Lenin and other Bolshevik leaders eventually led to his expulsion from the party in 1927.

Following his expulsion, Trotsky spent much of his time in exile, traveling to various countries in Europe and South America. He continued to write and speak out against the Soviet government, and his criticisms of Stalin's policies and the direction of the Soviet Union earned him many enemies.

In 1940, Trotsky was assassinated in Mexico City by a Stalinist agent. His death marked the end of an era in revolutionary politics, and his ideas on Marxism and revolutionary theory continue to influence socialist movements around the world.

Trotsky's legacy is a complex and controversial one. While he played a key role in the Bolshevik Revolution and helped shape the early years of the Soviet Union, his disagreements with Lenin and other Bolshevik leaders, as well as his criticisms of Stalin, ultimately led to his expulsion from the party and his eventual assassination.

Despite his flaws and the controversies surrounding his legacy, Trotsky remains an important figure in the history of socialist thought and revolutionary politics. His ideas on the role of the working class in revolutionary change, the need for international solidarity among socialists, and the importance of a vanguard party continue to inspire leftists and revolutionaries today.

THE BOLSHEVIK REVOLUTION AND THE FOUNDING OF THE SOVIET UNION

The Bolshevik Revolution of 1917 marked a turning point in Russian history. After the overthrow of the Tsarist regime, the Bolsheviks, led by Vladimir Lenin, established a socialist government and began the process of transforming Russia into a communist state. In 1922, the **Union of Soviet Socialist Republics (USSR)** was established, with Russia as its largest and most powerful member.

The Bolsheviks implemented a series of radical policies aimed at dismantling the old social, economic, and political order. Private property was abolished, and land was redistributed to peasants. Banks, factories, and other industries were nationalized, and the state took control of the economy. The Orthodox Church, long a pillar of Tsarist rule, was suppressed, and religion was replaced by a strict atheism.

The Bolsheviks faced fierce opposition from both domestic and foreign enemies, including anti-communist forces within Russia and foreign powers, such as Britain, France, and the United States. The resulting Civil War (1918-1922) was a devastating conflict that left millions dead and crippled the country's economy and infrastructure.

Despite these challenges, the Bolsheviks remained in power and set about creating a new Soviet society. They developed a system of government that was based on the principles of democratic centralism, which gave power to a centralized party leadership but also allowed for the participation of ordinary citizens in decision-making processes.

Under the Soviet government, Russia underwent a period of rapid industrialization and modernization. The Soviet economy was transformed from an agricultural-based system to an industrial one, with an emphasis on heavy industry and the development of key sectors such as steel, coal, and oil.

The Soviet government also pursued policies aimed at promoting equality and social justice. Education and healthcare were made available to all citizens, and women were granted equal rights and opportunities in society. The government also implemented policies aimed at eradicating illiteracy and improving the living standards of workers and peasants.

However, the Soviet regime was also characterized by repression and authoritarianism. Political dissent was not tolerated, and the government used a vast network of secret police and forced labor camps to suppress opposition. Stalin, who rose to power after Lenin's death in 1924, was responsible for the deaths of millions of people through purges and other forms of state violence.

Despite these challenges, the Soviet Union remained a superpower for much of the 20th century, and its influence was felt around the world. Its defeat of Nazi Germany in World War II cemented its status as a major global power, and it played a key role in the Cold War, the space race, and other international events.

In the late 1980s and early 1990s, however, the Soviet Union faced a series of internal and external pressures that ultimately led to its collapse. Economic stagnation, political dissent, and nationalist movements in various Soviet republics contributed to a growing sense of instability, and in 1991, the Soviet Union officially dissolved.

Today, Russia remains a major player on the global stage, with a rich history and culture that reflect its unique identity as a bridge between Europe and Asia. The legacy of the Soviet period continues to shape Russian society and politics, and the country continues to grapple with the challenges and opportunities of a rapidly changing world.

STALIN'S RULE AND THE RISE OF TOTALITARIANISM

Joseph Stalin was a Soviet politician and dictator who ruled the Soviet Union from the mid-1920s until his death in 1953. He played a central role in the Communist Party of the Soviet Union and implemented policies that resulted in the deaths of millions of people.

Stalin was born in 1878 in Georgia and joined the Bolshevik Party in 1912. He quickly rose through the party ranks and became General Secretary of the Central Committee in 1922. Stalin played a key role in consolidating power after the death of Vladimir Lenin in 1924 and established himself as the undisputed leader of the Soviet Union.

Stalin's policies focused on rapid industrialization and collectivization of agriculture. He implemented a series of Five-Year Plans, which aimed to transform the Soviet Union into an industrial powerhouse. Millions of peasants were forced off their land and into collective farms, and millions of workers were sent to labor camps to work on massive construction projects.

Stalin's regime was marked by widespread repression and violence. He implemented a system of purges, in which anyone suspected of opposing his regime was arrested, tortured, and executed. The purges targeted not only political opponents but also artists, intellectuals, and ordinary citizens. Estimates of the number of people killed during Stalin's reign range from **3 million to 20 million**.

Stalin's leadership during World War II was instrumental in the Soviet Union's victory over Nazi Germany. However, his regime continued to be characterized by brutality and repression even during the war. Stalin's paranoia led to the execution of many military officers and the imprisonment of millions of ordinary citizens on suspicion of disloyalty.

In the years after the war, Stalin's grip on power began to weaken. His policies of repression and violence had alienated many members of the Communist Party, and the Soviet economy was struggling to keep up with the demands of industrialization. Stalin's death in 1953 marked the end of an era in Soviet history.

Despite the atrocities committed under Stalin's rule, he remains a controversial figure in Russia. Some Russians still view him as a strong leader who modernized the Soviet Union and led the country to victory in World War II. Others see him as a brutal dictator who presided over one of the darkest periods in Russian history. Regardless of one's opinion of Stalin, it is clear that his policies and actions had a profound impact on the Soviet Union and the world.

WORLD WAR II AND THE GREAT PATRIOTIC WAR

World War II was one of the deadliest and most destructive conflicts in human history. It involved most of the world's nations, including the Soviet Union, which played a significant role in the war. The war marked a turning point in world history and had a profound impact on Russia's political and social landscape. The Soviet Union suffered the most casualties of any nation, with estimates ranging from 27 to 40 million people killed.

The Soviet Union entered the war in 1941, after Nazi Germany launched a massive invasion of the country. The invasion was part of Adolf Hitler's plan to conquer the Soviet Union and gain control over its vast resources. At first, the German army made significant gains, capturing many cities and advancing towards Moscow. However, the Soviet Union rallied and mounted a counteroffensive, which ultimately led to the defeat of the German army.

The Soviet Union's victory over Germany was a turning point in the war and a significant achievement for the country. The Great Patriotic War, as it was known in Russia, played a crucial role in shaping the nation's identity and national pride. It also marked the beginning of the Soviet Union's emergence as a superpower on the world stage.

During the war, the Soviet Union mobilized its economy and resources to support the war effort. The government implemented various policies and programs, including rationing and the mobilization of labor, to ensure that the country could sustain the war effort. The Soviet Union also received significant aid from its allies, including the United States, which provided military equipment and supplies to support the Soviet army.

The Soviet Union's victory over Nazi Germany was not without its costs. The war had a devastating impact on the country's infrastructure, economy, and population. Many cities and towns were destroyed, and millions of people were left homeless. The war also created significant political and social changes, as the Soviet Union emerged from the war as a superpower with new territories, including parts of Eastern Europe.

World War II and the Great Patriotic War had a significant impact on Russia's political, social, and economic landscape. The Soviet Union's victory over Nazi Germany played a critical role in shaping the nation's identity and national pride. It also marked the beginning of the Soviet Union's emergence as a superpower on the world stage. However, the war also had significant costs, including the loss of millions of lives and the destruction of infrastructure and the economy. The war created political and social changes that would shape Russia for decades to come.

KHRUSHCHEV'S THAW AND THE DE-STALINIZATION OF THE SOVIET UNION

During the mid-1950s, Nikita Khrushchev emerged as the leader of the Soviet Union, following the death of Joseph Stalin. Khrushchev brought about a period of political liberalization and cultural openness that became known as the "Thaw."

Khrushchev began the process of de-Stalinization, which involved the removal of Stalin's personality cult and the exposure of his brutal tactics. Khrushchev gave a speech at the 20th Communist Party Congress in 1956, in which he denounced Stalin's purges and crimes against humanity. This marked a significant departure from Stalin's policies and set the tone for the Thaw.

During the Thaw, there was a relaxation of censorship and an increase in artistic freedom. Writers, filmmakers, and artists were given more creative license, and they used it to explore previously taboo topics such as the horrors of Stalinism and the suffering of ordinary people. The Thaw also led to a rise in political dissent, with people openly criticizing the government and calling for more democratic reforms.

One of the most significant events of the Thaw was the 1962 **Cuban Missile Crisis**, which brought the world closer to nuclear war than ever before. Khrushchev's decision to install nuclear missiles in Cuba was a direct response to the United States' deployment of missiles in Turkey. The crisis was eventually resolved through diplomatic means, but it underscored the dangerous brinkmanship of the Cold War.

Despite Khrushchev's attempts at liberalization, his rule was not without controversy. His policies were often inconsistent, and he made several missteps, including the failed attempt to introduce corn as a major staple in the Soviet Union. He was also criticized for his handling of the economy, which suffered from stagnation and inefficiency.

Khrushchev's Thaw came to an end in 1964, when he was ousted from power by his own party. He was replaced by Leonid Brezhnev, who returned the Soviet Union to a more conservative and repressive stance. Nevertheless, the Thaw was an important period in Soviet history, and it paved the way for the later reforms of Mikhail Gorbachev in the 1980s.

Cuban Missile Crisis

The Cuban Missile Crisis was a pivotal moment in the history of the Cold War and one of the most tense moments in the relationship between the United States and the Soviet Union. It occurred in October of 1962, when the Soviet Union installed nuclear missiles in Cuba, which posed a direct threat to the security of the United States.

The background to the crisis was the ongoing hostility between the United States and the Soviet Union, who were locked in a Cold War that had been simmering since the end of World War II. The Soviet Union had been alarmed by the United States' deployment of missiles in Turkey, and decided to retaliate by placing missiles in Cuba, which was seen as a strategic location that would allow the Soviet Union to target major US cities with nuclear weapons.

The US became aware of the missile deployment in Cuba in October 1962, and President John F. Kennedy ordered a naval blockade of Cuba to prevent further Soviet shipments of missiles. Tensions rose rapidly, and the world was on the brink of nuclear war.

Both sides engaged in intense diplomatic negotiations, and after several days of tense negotiations, a deal was reached in which the Soviet Union agreed to remove its missiles from Cuba in exchange for a US pledge not to invade Cuba and to remove US missiles from Turkey.

The Cuban Missile Crisis had far-reaching consequences for both the United States and the Soviet Union. It marked a turning point in the Cold War, as both sides recognized the dangers of nuclear war and became more cautious in their approach to international relations. It also demonstrated the power of diplomacy and the importance of communication between world leaders.

For the Soviet Union, the crisis was a humiliation and a setback in their efforts to expand their influence around the world. For the United States, it was a victory that bolstered the country's reputation as a global superpower.

The Cuban Missile Crisis remains a powerful reminder of the dangers of nuclear war and the importance of diplomacy in resolving conflicts. It serves as a warning that the use of nuclear weapons could have catastrophic consequences for the entire world, and that leaders must work together to prevent such a catastrophic event from occurring.

BREZHNEV'S STAGNATION AND THE END OF THE COLD WAR

During the 1970s, the Soviet Union was led by Leonid Brezhnev, a leader who sought to maintain the status quo and maintain the country's power in the face of internal and external pressures. This period became known as the era of stagnation, as economic growth slowed and social progress stagnated.

Brezhnev's policy of détente, or a reduction in tensions with the West, continued under his leadership. This was marked by a series of arms control agreements, including the Strategic Arms Limitation Talks (SALT) with the United States. However, the Soviet Union's military buildup continued, leading to a dangerous arms race with the US.

Internally, Brezhnev's leadership was marked by a lack of political and economic reforms, leading to stagnation in the country's development. The economy was heavily centralized and bureaucratic, with little innovation or creativity. Corruption and inefficiency were rampant, leading to a decline in living standards and a rise in social discontent.

Despite this stagnation, there were signs of change in the Soviet Union. The country was becoming more diverse, with a growing middle class and a more educated population. Dissent was also growing, with writers and intellectuals challenging the Soviet system and calling for greater freedoms and human rights.

In the 1980s, the Soviet Union saw a period of dramatic change under the leadership of Mikhail Gorbachev. Gorbachev launched a series of reforms aimed at revitalizing the Soviet economy and political system, known as perestroika and glasnost.

Perestroika involved decentralizing the economy and allowing greater market forces to operate, while glasnost aimed to increase transparency and openness in Soviet society. This led to greater freedom of speech and the press, and a loosening of state control over cultural and artistic expression.

However, these reforms also brought unintended consequences, including a weakening of central authority and a rise in ethnic tensions. The Soviet Union's satellite states in Eastern Europe began to break away, leading to the fall of the Berlin Wall in 1989 and the eventual collapse of the Soviet Union in 1991.

Brezhnev's stagnation and Gorbachev's reforms marked the end of the Soviet era and the beginning of a new chapter in Russian history. The Soviet Union's collapse led to a period of political and economic turmoil, but also opened the door to new opportunities and freedoms for the Russian people.

THE COLLAPSE OF THE SOVIET UNION AND THE EMERGENCE OF RUSSIA AS A NEW STATE

The collapse of the Soviet Union in 1991 marked the end of an era and the beginning of a new one in Russian history. The country had undergone significant changes since the fall of the Tsarist regime in 1917, and the subsequent rise and fall of communism. The Soviet Union had been a superpower, and its dissolution marked the end of the Cold War and the beginning of a new chapter in global politics.

The collapse of the Soviet Union was a complex process that involved economic, political, and social factors. The country had been facing economic problems for years, including a stagnant economy, a declining standard of living, and shortages of basic goods. The government's attempts to reform the economy in the 1980s had failed, leading to widespread discontent among the population.

Political reforms, such as the introduction of a multiparty system and the establishment of a new constitution, were also attempted in the 1980s and early 1990s. However, these reforms were not enough to save the Soviet Union from collapse. The political system was plagued by corruption, inefficiency, and a lack of transparency, leading to widespread disillusionment among the population.

Social factors also played a significant role in the collapse of the Soviet Union. Nationalism had been growing among the Soviet republics for years, and many people felt that their cultural identity was being suppressed by the centralized government in Moscow. The Baltic republics were the first to declare independence, followed by other republics, including Ukraine and Belarus.

The collapse of the Soviet Union was also marked by a power struggle between the reformers and hardliners within the Communist Party. Mikhail Gorbachev, who had been instrumental in introducing reforms, was ousted in a coup in 1991. The coup failed, and Boris Yeltsin emerged as the new leader of Russia.

The collapse of the Soviet Union was a turning point in Russian history. The country had to undergo a difficult transition from a centralized planned economy to a market economy. The 1990s were marked by economic turmoil, political instability, and social unrest. The privatization of state assets led to the emergence of a new class of oligarchs, who wielded significant economic and political power.

Russia's relationship with the West also changed after the collapse of the Soviet Union. The country became more integrated into the global economy, and there were attempts to establish closer ties with the West. However, relations with the United States and Europe have been strained at times, particularly over issues such as NATO expansion and conflicts in the Balkans and the Middle East.

The collapse of the Soviet Union also had significant geopolitical implications. The country's role as a superpower had come to an end, and the United States emerged as the world's sole superpower. The collapse of the Soviet Union also led to the emergence of new independent states, including Ukraine, Belarus, and the Baltic republics.

The collapse of the Soviet Union marked the end of an era in Russian history. The country underwent significant changes, including a transition to a market economy and the emergence of a new political and economic elite. The collapse of the Soviet Union also had significant geopolitical implications, leading to the emergence of new independent states and changes in the global balance of power.

PUTIN'S ERA AND THE RESURGENCE OF RUSSIAN POWER

Vladimir Putin was born in Leningrad (now known as St. Petersburg), Russia on October 7, 1952. His father was a factory foreman and his mother was a factory worker, and Putin was raised in a communal apartment with other families. Putin was interested in sports from a young age, and he was particularly good at judo.

After finishing high school, Putin attended Leningrad State University, where he studied law. After graduating, he joined the KGB, the Soviet Union's security agency, and worked as a spy in East Germany for several years.

During the height of the Cold War, Vladimir Putin was posted to East Germany as a KGB agent in the early 1980s. He was stationed in Dresden, a city located in the German Democratic Republic (GDR), which was a Soviet satellite state at the time.

Putin's job in Dresden was to gather intelligence on Western nations, particularly the United States. He was part of a group of KGB officers known as the "illegal residents" who were tasked with carrying out covert operations to support Soviet interests in the region.

As part of his duties, Putin established a network of informants and developed a deep understanding of the political and economic landscape of the GDR. He also cultivated relationships with key officials in the

Communist Party of East Germany and gained valuable insights into the workings of the East German government. Putin's time in East Germany coincided with a period of significant political and social upheaval in the country. In 1989, as the Soviet Union began to crumble, protests erupted throughout the GDR calling for political reform and an end to the country's one-party rule.

Despite being a KGB agent, Putin was sympathetic to the pro-democracy movements that were sweeping through Eastern Europe. He recognized that change was coming and advocated for a peaceful transition to democracy in East Germany.

After the fall of the Berlin Wall in 1989, Putin was recalled to Moscow. He continued to work for the KGB and its successor agency, the Federal Security Service (FSB), rising through the ranks to become director of the FSB in 1998.

After the collapse of the Soviet Union, Putin returned to Russia and became involved in politics.

In 1999, Putin was appointed as the Prime Minister of Russia by then-President Boris Yeltsin. Yeltsin resigned on December 31, 1999, and Putin became acting President. He won the presidential election in March 2000 and was re-elected in 2004 and 2012.

Putin's leadership has been marked by a resurgence of Russian power on the international stage and the consolidation of his grip on domestic politics.

During his early years in power, Putin focused on restoring Russia's economy and political stability. He implemented reforms aimed at improving Russia's business climate and attracting foreign investment, and succeeded in stabilizing the Russian ruble after the economic turbulence of the 1990s.

At the same time, Putin sought to assert Russian influence in the former Soviet republics, which he referred to as Russia's "near abroad." In 2008, Russia fought a brief war with Georgia over the breakaway region of South Ossetia, which Russia ultimately recognized as an independent state. This move was widely condemned by the international community, but it cemented Russia's status as a regional power.

Putin has also been known for his crackdown on political opposition and the media. He has been accused of suppressing dissent and restricting freedom of speech, particularly in the lead-up to elections. In 2012, Putin was elected to a third term as President, despite allegations of election fraud and widespread protests.

Putin's foreign policy has been characterized by a desire to reassert Russian influence on the global stage. He has sought to challenge the dominance of the United States and the European Union, and has pursued closer ties with China and other emerging powers. Under Putin's leadership, Russia has become increasingly assertive in its foreign policy, particularly in the Middle East.

In 2014, Russia annexed the Ukrainian peninsula of Crimea, which had been part of Ukraine since 1954. The move was widely condemned by the international community, and led to a deterioration in relations between Russia and the West. The conflict in eastern Ukraine, which began in the wake of the annexation, has claimed over 10,000 lives and remains ongoing.

In 2022, Russia invaded Ukraine again starting a war in Europe that has been last back in the Second World War, creating instability not only in Europe, but around the world.

Despite Russia's international isolation and economic challenges, Putin remains popular among many Russians. He has been praised for his role in restoring Russian pride and prestige, and for his efforts to modernize the country's economy and military.

Looking to the future, Putin's legacy remains uncertain. While he has been able to consolidate power and assert Russian influence on the global stage, his authoritarian tendencies and crackdown on dissent have raised concerns about the long-term prospects for democracy and political freedom in Russia. Nevertheless, Putin's era has been a transformative period in Russian history, and one that will continue to shape the country's trajectory for years to come.

REFLECTIONS ON RUSSIA'S PAST AND FUTURE PROSPECTS

As we come to the end of this brief history of Russia, it's important to reflect on the country's past and consider its future prospects. Russia has a rich and complex history, filled with both triumphs and tragedies, and it has played a significant role in shaping the world as we know it today.

From its early days as Kievan Rus to its time under Mongol rule, the emergence of Moscow as a dominant power, the reigns of the Romanovs, the tumultuous years of the Time of Troubles, the westernization of Russia under Peter the Great, the cultural blossoming under Catherine the Great, the struggles for reform and revolution in the 19th and 20th centuries, and the rise and fall of the Soviet Union, Russia's history is a fascinating and intricate tapestry.

Looking to the future, it's clear that Russia faces many challenges and opportunities. In recent years, Russia under the leadership of President Vladimir Putin has reasserted its influence on the global stage, pursuing an assertive foreign policy and investing heavily in its military and defense capabilities.

At the same time, Russia faces significant economic and social challenges, including an aging population, low productivity, and widespread corruption. There are also concerns about the state of democracy and civil liberties in the country, as well as the impact of environmental degradation and climate change.

Despite these challenges, there are reasons to be hopeful about Russia's future. The country has a rich cultural heritage and a highly educated population, with a strong tradition of innovation and entrepreneurship. There are also signs of increasing civic engagement and activism, particularly among young people.

As Russia continues to navigate the complex geopolitical landscape of the 21st century, it will be important for the country to balance its global ambitions with a commitment to addressing domestic challenges and promoting inclusive economic growth and development. It will also be essential to foster a more open and transparent political system that allows for greater participation and accountability.

Russia's history is a testament to the resilience and determination of its people, who have overcome tremendous challenges and made significant contributions to the world. As we look to the future, there is much to be hopeful about, and it's clear that Russia will continue to play an important role in shaping the course of history.

....
END.

Made in the USA
Monee, IL
07 March 2024

54616703R00046